IMAGES
of England

SHEPTON MALLET

Jubilee Celebrations, 6 May 1935. 'From the Waterloo Road Schools to the Cenotaph and extending into Collett Park the streets resembled a veritable fairyland.' The advent of electricity to the town made floodlights possible for the first time and the church, Market Cross and cenotaph were floodlit from Saturday until Monday. A grand procession was held and one of the winning trade exhibits was Charlton Brewery's 'Beer is Best'.

IMAGES
of England

SHEPTON MALLET

Compiled by
Fred Davis

TEMPUS

First published 2001
Copyright © Fred Davis, 2001

Tempus Publishing Limited
The Mill, Brimscombe Port,
Stroud, Gloucestershire, GL5 2QG

ISBN 0 7524 2197 2

Typesetting and origination by
Tempus Publishing Limited
Printed in Great Britain by
Midway Colour Print, Wiltshire

Children of Victoria Grove dressed up to dance around the maypole, on the Charlton Brewery lorry entered in the Shepton Mallet Carnival around 1930. From left to right, back row: B. Blacker, A. Boyce, G. Cooper, G. Youdle, F. Youdle, K. Cooper, H. Hutchings, L. Foxwell (a sister of H. Hutchings). Front row: M. Sparks, F. Witmore, H. Blacker, K. Boyce, J. Blinman. The three smaller ones are unknown.

Contents

Acknowledgments   6

Introduction   7

1.   The Town Centre   9

2.   Industry   27

3.   Agriculture   45

4.   Church and Education   53

5.   Institutions   61

6.   Recreation   67

7.   The War Years   77

8.   Special Occasions   81

9.   A Changing Townscape   95

10. Around Shepton Mallet   105

Acknowledgements

This publication was made possible only with the help and support of many people, both in Shepton Mallet and the surrounding villages. Particular thanks must go to Richard Rainsford, our village historian for providing many of the postcards and research on the villages.

The book could not have been completed without the patience and encouragement of my wife Pat. The technical support of my son Edward Davis was essential in scanning postcards onto computer disks; this made possible the fast and accurate copying of valuable pictures without the risk of loss or damage. My brother Roy Davis sifted through hundreds of postcards and photographs in order to make this selection.

Market Place, Shepton, Mallet, 1923.

Introduction

Set in an area of outstanding natural beauty, Shepton Mallet nestles in a narrow combe on the southern slopes of the Mendip Hills. Outwardly the impression is of a sleepy market town; but nothing could be further from the truth. For some 5,000 years settlers have been attracted to the Shepton Mallet area. Their presence etched in the surrounding landscape are visible reminders of long forgotten ages. An Iron Age Hill Fort dominates the northern side of the town, and a little to the east, on the crest of Beacon Hill, is a scatter of round-barrows indicating the political, ceremonial and religious importance of this area.

The Roman Fosse Road passes the eastern end of the town. Built in a more-or-less straight line from Exeter to Lincoln in an endless ribbon of stone, it is an indelible mark on the English landscape as clear today as it was almost 2,000 years ago. It was here in recent years, that a substantial Roman settlement was uncovered. In what was described as a Christian burial ground a Chi Rho Amulet was unearthed, so providing proof-positive of the earliest Christian burial in Britain – pre-dating St Augustin by some two hundred years.

Unlike its near-neighbours, ecclesiastical Wells or that cradle of Christianity, Glastonbury, Shepton Mallet is, and always has been an industrial town that is clearly marked in its medieval townscape and fine buildings. Narrow cobbled walks flanked by high grey-stoned walls meander past an essentially Norman (though its Saxon beginnings are still clear) church, then suddenly careering into the valley below, skirting sombre walls of the oldest working prison in the country, built in 1620 as a House of Correction.

Throughout the valley of the River Sheppey, grand mansion houses and more humble cottages echo a time when Shepton's fortunes were at their peak during the prosperous days of the West Country Woollen Industry. The towns' growth and prosperity was built on the woollen industry and large flocks of sheep were grazed on the sleights overlooking the town. This led to the naming of the settlement as Sceap-Fold, Sheeptun, Shepton.

The Norman invasion of 1066 brought into William the Conqueror's retinue a Knight named William Mallet and among his many grants of lands was Shepton, to which he appended his name making Shepton Mallet among one of the earliest double place names. One of the oldest market towns in Somerset, Shepton was granted its first market charter in 1219. The market place was the commercial and social hub of the town and focal point for the surrounding villages. The first blood of the Civil War in these parts was shed here (1642); and rebels were hung drawn and quartered (1685) from the Market Cross.

A set of Shambles (from Anglo Saxon 'Scamel' or 'Little Bench') still remain as a reminder of better days when buyers from across the country came here to purchase quality woollen cloth.

Elizabethan documents show Shepton products finding their way abroad; to Bilbao and St Sesbastion, for example, in bundles of ten cloths; light popinjay greens, light sky colours and fine stamell reds among other shades. Though the main commodity sold was wool, other more dainty items were also put up for sale. During the early nineteenth century the last wife was sold in the Market Place. She was 'knocked down for half a crown complete with halter round her neck'. For three hundred years the valley of the Sheppey hummed with life till the first crack of the whip of doom sounded with the industrial revolution. Nearly all Shepton's trade had departed by 1839. The introduction of silk and crape kept some employment going for a time but this declined also.

The technological advances during the nineteenth century, particularly that brought about by the introduction of steam power, precipitated violent reaction in the West Country Woollen Industry, yet it also inspired the development of large centralised breweries such as Oakhill (founded 1767), Charlton (1844), and the Anglo-Bavarian Brewery (1864). And on a much smaller scale was the Showering's Brewery at Kilver Street, which they purchased in 1843. This in turned helped to alleviate the very suffering caused by opposition to the new technology.

Shepton's strength remains its strong industrial base. Historically the town has always been resilient. When the Huguenot weavers succumbed to the Industrial Revolution, the brewers arrived. When the cattle market left the town, in came light industry. The Golden Age of Babycham passed and the international Fashion Company Mulberry made Kilver Court their headquarters. Clark's shoes left the town and were replaced by Dr Martins. British Telecom is here as are Huntsman's Polyurethane's and the Internet Company, UK On Line. Nor has alcohol been abandoned: a north-east wind still wafts the sweet tang of fermenting apples across the town from Matthew Clark's cider factory, with a proud boast of being Europe's premier cider plant. And at the Anglo Trading Estate, Brothers Drinks is run by four brothers; the great nephews of Francis Showing, inventor of Babycham. There the brothers run a 24-hour shift system with a bottling capacity of some one million bottles a week. The old Charlton Brewery and Anglo Trading Estate houses a wide range of industries from high tech to general engineering; a diversity that will enable Shepton Mallet to step confidently into the new millennium. Shepton Mallet is proud of its history, and confident of its future. It is indeed a town with a past and future to envy.

Fred Davis
January 2001

One
The Town Centre

The Market Place has witnessed many colourful and turbulent scenes. The first blood of the English Civil War in the area was spilt here, and later, in 1685, several good Sheptonians were hung, drawn and quartered for their part in the Monmouth Rebellion. On market days men and women were locked in the stocks for various misdemeanours.

The Market Place, *c.* 1890. The large arcaded building was the Lamb Inn, a coaching inn that boasted stabling for one hundred horses. Beneath the arches hung huge Beam Scales from which bales of wool were weighed on market days. The cottages in the background served to enclose the churchyard, which was entered by a small arch at the left end of the row of cottages.

The Shambles (from Anglo Saxon 'scamel' or 'little bench') on the north side of the Market Place, were taken down in 1912. The Shambles once lined the north and south side of the Market Place and on market days were the sole preserve of the butchers where freshly killed country meat was sold.

Long before dawn, the dark shapes of pack horses would pick their precarious way over the ill-kept roads of Mendip and selected their pitch in the Market Place – a weekly routine unbroken since around 1219, when the town was first granted a Market Charter.

Mr Butler's harness shop in the Market Place. The family-run shop was famed for having made the harness that was placed around the neck of the last woman to be sold in the Market Place. She was knocked down for half a crown, complete with halter around her neck!

Singlestick Match – a game of Single Stick in progress in the Market Place in front of the Bunch of Grapes Inn, around 1820. Although serious wounds could be inflicted, the game was often played for a small wager such as a new hat!

The Black Swan, Market Place, affectionately known as 'Sot's Hole'. The Showering family owned it for some years before they moved to the Ship Inn at Kilver Street where they became known world-wide for the Perry drink Babycham.

The official unveiling of the water fountain in the Market Place during December 1868. It was paid for by public subscription, and the Shepton Mallet Gas and Water Companies supplied the gas and water free of charge. From left to right: Mr F. Cottrill, Richard Burt Jnr, Robert North, J.H. Day, -?-.

The Black Swan and council building taken from below the arches of the Market Cross during the late 1960s.

The George Inn in the Market Place, now the Midland Bank.

The Market Cross was built in 1500 by Walter Buckland, a wealthy clothier, as a memorial to his wife Agnes.

Town Street, Shepton Mallet looking north. *c.* 1900.

Advertisement for Royal Balsamic Plaisters.

Town Street, *c*. 1890. Postman Davies stands under the copper kettle of 'Tinman' Allen's shop. Mr Allen was well-known for his musical abilities and played in many local orchestras and concerts.

Town Street looking south, *c*. 1900.

Mr 'Tinman' Allen poses outside his shop in Town Street, c. 1900. He was renowned for the manufacture of a wide variety of tools and utensils, a display of which can be found in the Gloucester Folk Museum.

Mr Allen travelled a wide area selling his wares at markets and fairs and is seen here posing outside his tent.

The Co-operative Stores, Town Street, c. 1912. As a child I would stare spellbound as the customer's change was placed in small metal containers and would zoom along overhead wires, reaching its destination with a loud ding. This shop was demolished during the early 1970s. The site forms part of the town's inner relief road.

The Red Lion Inn, Market Place in 1920.

Edith Moon (left) and two year old Ella Moon (to Edith's right) with friends, posing outside No. 9 Town Street in 1909. The shop (later Frisby's) is decorated to celebrate the visit of the Prince and Princess of Wales.

Town Street, looking south prior to town centre redevelopment in the late 1960s.

Waterloo Road viewed from Town Street during the 1960s and just prior to redevelopment of the area.

High Street, Shepton Mallet, looking north in 1904.

High Street looking north, 1904.

High Street, Shepton Mallet, 1904.

High Street looking south, 1908.

High Street, Shepton Mallet, 1910.

Shepton Mallet High Street during the 1960s.

High Street with the Railway Inn on the right and Venture Café on the left in the 1960s.

Advertisment for Fred J. Parker.

Two
Industry

Middle Darshill Cloth Factory, *c.* 1900. This was just one of some thirty mills that straddled the tiny river in the valley of Sheppey. This mill produced the silk for Queen Victoria's wedding gown and was the last to cease production in the town around 1912.

Grandmother Jacobs pictured outside No. 24 Darshill around 1910 with her bobbin winder. Mrs Jacobs was an 'outworker' for the Middle Darshill Silk Mill that stood in the valley below her home. The children are Tom and Elsie Tutton.

Monmouth House, so called as the Duke of Monmouth's men are said to have stayed there during their excursions through the town prior to the fateful battle of Sedgemoor. The mansion house later became the Co-operative bakery and was home of the popular 'Sixpenny Hops' at weekends until it was demolished to make way for the Hillmead Flats development in the mid-1960s.

A 'Dark Satanic Mill' at the rear of Monmouth House, c. 1962.

Kilver Street, just one of several quite separate industrial communities that owes its early development to the rural Woollen Industry. It was originally grouped around the great fulling mills that straddled the fast flowing stream on which it depended for its motive power.

Daddy Fisher's Lane. This photograph probably best depicts the density of dwellings in the industrial valley. At the height of the woollen industry it is said that some 5,000 souls were directly employed in the staple industry and they were all crammed into Shepton's narrow industrial valley.

Leg Street's junction with Peter Street. Until 1912 a small footbridge offered an alternative to wading through the ford. On the right are the remains of the town mill, put to the torch in the early 1800s, then incorporated into Mr Sherring's Brewery and finally demolished around 1912 when the local authority opened up Leg Street and created the 'Leg Square' that we know today.

The Anglo Bavarian Brewery reputed to be the first lager brewery in the United Kingdom. It was erected in 1860 as an export brewery and brewed a light beer in the Bavarian style, not unlike the present day lager. The erection of the brewery came at a time when the textile industry locally had seriously declined and offered new hope for employment prospects in the town.

Coopers of the Anglo Bavarian Brewery during the Jubilee Celebrations.

The cask washing department at the Anglo.

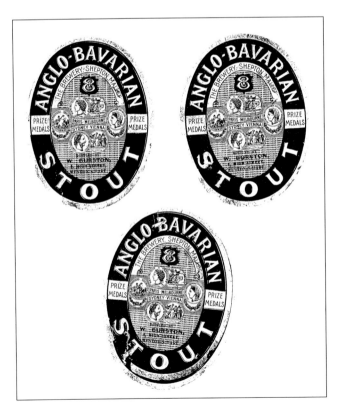

Anglo Bavarian bottle labels.

The Anglo Bavarian Brewery had its own fire brigade and provided the only effective fire cover for the town from 1868 until the brewery closed in 1921. This photograph is taken at the rear of the brewery around 1909. The captain (in the driving seat) is Mr Charles Mitchel. A visiting brigade is on the left.

Members of the Anglo Fire Brigade, They were winners of almost every competition, and among the most modern in the country. Some of those pictured are: Archie Garton (with his dog Puck), Fred Bown, Mr Green, Reg Allen, Mr Wollen, Mr Austin and Mr Stone.

The Shepton Mallet Fire Brigade in Charlton Road, Shepton Mallet, celebrating the Coronation of Edward V11, 1902.

An exhibition by the Anglo Apple Mills at the Shepton Mallet Agricultural Show, *c*. 1955.

The interior of the Anglo Apple Mill at Darshill, Shepton Mallet.

Feeding the apples into the mill at the Darshill factory.

The name Showering and Babycham are synonymous with Shepton Mallet. The Showering family had been involved in brewing in the town for almost two hundred years and won a world-wide reputation for their cider and Perry drinks. The photo was taken outside the Ship Inn at Kilver Street in 1933 and shows Showering's representatives on their motor cycles.

The 1950s were the golden days of Babycham. The new drink won first prize at every major agricultural show in the country. In addition associated companies won gold medals in all the post war Brewer's Exhibitions. Pictured is Miss Kathleen (daughter of Herbert Showering) with one of the winning entries before leaving for the Brewer's Exhibition in 1953. From left to right: Mr Francis, Herbert, Kathleen, Ralph, Mr Arthur Showering.

Babycham advertisement, 1983.

Unloading trucks of apples at High Street Station, Shepton Mallet. From the foreground back: H. Allen, C. Rymes, A. Carter, G. Lumber, Jim Weeks, K. Lumber, B. Roberts, Mr A Showering, C. Smart, Keith Showering, Mr Herbert Showering, Mr Trym, T. Lintern, J. Wallace, Herbert Boyce.

The Maltings at Charlton Brewery and its weed-covered millpond before it was redeveloped.

The site of the Charlton Brewery was transformed into a successful industrial estate by local developers, Dennis and Sue Dennett. The original millpond now acts as a central focal point.

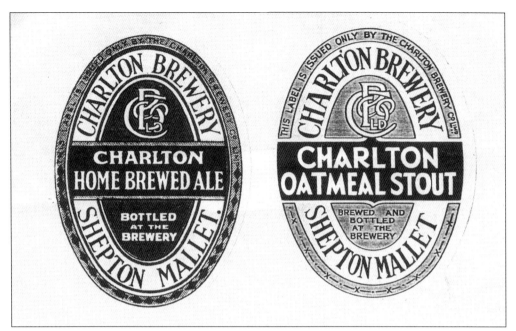

Bottle labels for Charlton beers.

Group of workers at Charlton Brewery. From left to right: T. Ware, B. Hann, E. Thick, B. Benjamin (at rear), Cox, Mr F. Youdle.

Interior of the Cooper's Shop at Charlton.

Charlton Brewery lorry. From left to right: B. Benjamin, T. Ware, F. Youdle.

Stone has been quarried in the Mendips for the past 2,000 years and remains an important local industry. The photograph, taken at Waterlip Quarry, dates from a time when stone was extracted by hand and transported by horse and cart. Stone was taken to the Shepton Prison where it was broken down by hand as a hard labour task, or to the workhouse for tramps to break up in return for a nights board.

A new stone crusher being installed at Windsor Hill Quarry, Shepton Mallet by John Wainwright & Co Ltd, *c.* 1900.

During the nineteenth century a cobweb of tramlines spread over the Mendips linking newly acquired stone quarries.

A group of quarry workers at Wainwright's quarry with drills, sledgehammers and other tools of their labours.

Shorter journeys were made by steam lorries capable of carrying six tons of stone which led to extensive surface damage to the local roads.

Drilling the face at Callow Rock Lime Quarry, Cheddar.

A loaded steam lorry leaves Callow Rock Lime Quarry at Cheddar.

One of many steam lorries which plied the roads of Mendip during the early years of the century. Their range was limited and the damage to the roads often unacceptable, therefore greater use was made of the new rail system.

Three
Agriculture

During the week of the annual Shepton Mallet Agricultural Show, the vanity fair came to town. The horse-drawn caravans would trundle into Cooks Paddock several days before the show and line up along the wall of Petticoat Lane. Each caravan doubled as a side-show; perhaps a shooting gallery or coconut shies.

The Steam Roundabout was only one of many attractions at the vanity fair. Others included a 'Freak Show' (often a Fat Lady who screamed out for you to come and feel her arms, to confirm they were real!) and a boxing booth that was a focal point for local pugilists and bullies – many half-drunk.

Captain Bond outside his harness shop in Commercial Road. He was a member of the several musical groups in the town and gave tuition on the trumpet.

One of many decorated arches that were erected to celebrate the annual Shepton Mallet Agricultural Show. Annie Godfrey said: 'The photographer has just asked when the arch would be ready. I said, Not until tomorrow morning. He said, Oh, but you won't be here. I said, No, I don't intend to be in it. He went straight ahead behind my back and this is the result. It is composed of poppies, corn and apples – lovely'.

Entrance to Shepton Mallet Show Field opposite Field Villas, c. 1904.

High Street decorated for Shepton Show.

One of the many attractions at the Shepton Show, c. 1970.

Judging the sheep at Shepton Show, c. 1937.

Young farmer Hoddinot inspects the pig entries at the show, c. 1938.

The Cattle Market around 1904, was held on the site of the (now) Shepton Mallet Motors. It would attract up to 300-400 head of cattle, illustrating the district's strong agricultural influence. Before the days of road transport the cattle would be herded along the towns' mud-strewn streets by drovers.

Ookey Thomas, a nineteenth century drover. He was a local character and was said to have lived among the willow beds where the Ridgeway Estate now is. Ookey was typical of his kind and found an abundance of work herding cattle, sheep, and even geese.

The weekly calf market, which was held in the field just over the GWR Bridge, where calves, sometimes less than a day old were bought and sold. It is now the site of the Ridgeway Housing Estate.

Railway sidings at the High Street (GWR) Station around 1890, where the cattle were loaded after being driven from the Cattle Market at the top of town.

Left: Farmer Norman and friends waiting to load the cattle onto trucks at High Street Station. *Right:* Mrs Louise Peeters is pictured with the horse and putt that was used to empty dustbins throughout the town in 1927.

High Street station in the 1920s.

Four
Church and Education

William and George Strode, wealthy local clothiers, founded the old grammar school in 1672. The school served the town for over 250 years and finally closed in 1899. It is now used as the rectory.

The Grammar School in Charlton Road opened in 1902 as a replacement for the old school founded in 167?. This one finally closed in 1918 and is now a leisure centre on the Whitstone School Campus.

Waterloo Road Infants' School, 1912.

Waterloo Road School, *c.* 1930.

Waterloo Road Girls School, 1923-1924. The pupils include: Violet Maidment, Dorothy Smith, Marjorie Slocombe, Lil Smith, Gwen Sheer, Murial Lovering, Phylis Pippard, Dulcie Hann, Nan Osborne, Daisy Colston, Nellie Bond, ? Hinks, Doris Mills, Hilda Barnes, Maude Collins, Elsie Achiells, Ella Cooper, Maud Ladd, Florie Wooley, ? Bull, ? Thomas. The teacher is Hilda Beard.

Bowlish schoolboys, in 1917. From left to right: Alec Baker, Walter Price, George Allen, Stan Reader, Fred Rolls, Willie Reader, Tom Tutton, Miss Alsop, Miss Fear, Erine Gardener, David Gunn, Jack Manship, Walter Burchell, George Manship, Arthur Norman, Bert Lambert, Vic Reader, Jack Drew, Bert Moon, John Peck, Fred Manship, Harold Gumm.

Church Lane, Shepton Mallet.

Left: Church Lane offers one of several intimate glimpses of the parish church of St Peter and St Paul. The church contains remnants of its Saxon origins whilst the Norman tower dates from around 1381. It is said to be one of the finest church towers in Somerset.

Below opposite: Parish Church Youth Fellowship, *c.* 1947. From left to right, back row: John Cocket, Audrey Lenthal, Dennis Lockey, Mary Swain, Ron Rossiter, Rita Buckingham, Doreen Higgins, Cliff Ryall, Sylvia Higgins. Centre row: Derek Marshman, Rosemary Rendell, Michael Baker, Pat Male, Jean Grist, Mary Miles, June Green, Beryl Lilley, Olive Bailey, Brenda Bailey, Rita Stock, Ruth Stock, Violet Higgins, Sheila Wilton. Front row: Bernice Shaw, John Swain, Nancy Stevens, Revd Rees-Jones, -?-, Ray Lockey, Audrey Thomas, John Moon.

Above left: The interior of the parish church has several fine features including walls of the original Saxon Nave, a Saxon Font, double Piscina and an effigy of one of the Mallet family who gave Shepton the second part of its name. But probably the most famous is the roof of the clerestory. It has 350 panels carved with tracery designs, and no two are the same.

Above right: The late fifteenth century stone pulpit in Shepton Mallet Parish Church.

The parish church dominates the centre of the town in this picture taken from The Batch in the 1880s.

The date 6 August 1908 was a very special day in the life of Mr Silas Davis when he was presented with the Imperial Service Medal, the first to be presented to the Postal Service.

Post Office workers, *c.* 1900.

Following in his father's footsteps, Ernest
Davis, born 1 June 1884.

'Number Please'. When Mr A.J. Reeves took over the Oakhill Post Office in 1922 there were just fourteen telephone subscribers. Their day started at 4.55 a.m. and finished at 8.00 p.m. The scale of payment was £76 6s per annum with a further £33 18s for working the telephone exchange. This photograph was taken in August 1949, courtesy of Mr M. Reeves.

Printed application for post of sub-postmaster, 21 December 1921.

Five

Institutions

Shepton Mallet Prison. The casual visitor stares in awe at the sombre aspect of its towering grey stone walls which, for over three centuries have served to incarcerate the most trivial to the most notorious offenders. It is the oldest working prison in the country and was erected in 1627 at a cost of just £230. Masons working on this grim development were paid 5d a day (less than two new pence) and labourers received 3½ old pence.

PRISON ENTRANCE, SHEPTON MALLET.

The main entrance to the prison where in darker days it was common to be hanged for petty stealing. One man received capital punishment for stealing a watch at Taunton, and in the same year a boy received the death sentence for the theft of a handkerchief from a village dance. However the boy won a reprieve – deportation for life!

Governor and staff of the prison, c. 1912. In 1930 the prison was closed and it looked as though it had reached the end of its useful life. Later on during the war, part of it was used as a repository for the Nation Archives including the Doomsday Book. The Americans used another part as a Military Detention barracks, followed later by the British Army. So it remained until early 1966 when again the prisons' future was in doubt. However, in June 1966 its gates again clanged shut on the first twenty-five civilian prisoners and so it remains today.

Public Record Office, Shepton Mallet: During the Second World War a section of the prison became home for the National Archives. Some 300 tons of records were stored there including such documents as the Doomsday Book and the log of *HMS Victory*, with Nelson's name heading the casualty list. Pictured is Mr Collie, a repairer of documents making his daily check on the archives.

The Norah Fry Hospital, erected in 1848 as a Union Workhouse on the site of an earlier one (built in 1700). Although this regime ended in 1930 when it was taken over by the County Council as a home for mentally defective women, in the minds of many it was still the dreaded workhouse, striking fear in the hearts of the working class poor. Norah Fry Hospital finally closed on 30 June 1993 under a new strategy of 'Care in the Community'.

Left: Matron of the workhouse, *c.* 1913.
Right: Master of the workhouse, *c.* 1913.

Shepton Mallet District Hospital. During the latter half of the nineteenth century there was a great surge of benevolence to provide hospitals. Many of them started life in houses and gave rise to the term 'Cottage Hospital'. In Shepton, the first such hospital was established in 1869. In 1879 the District Hospital was created, funded by private subscription. It has now been converted into private dwellings.

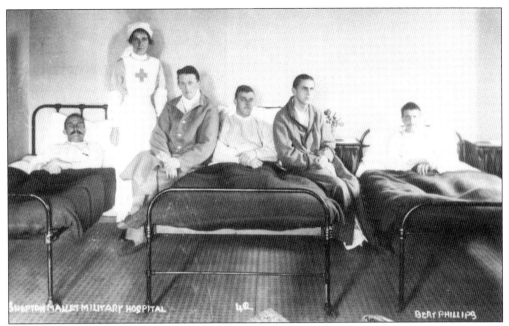

During the First World War the Red Cross took over a large ward which was originally a children's ward and also the house next door as a Military Convalescent Hospital. The picture shows some staff and patients there during 1916.

Patients and staff of the Shepton Mallet Military Hospital, 1916. Names include Brown, Pearce, Harregain, Cloan, Poole, Handford, Day, Oliver, Leaman, Peach, Howe, Halt, Gould, Cowling, Harlow, Buckle, Chapman, Pacey, Houseden, Slack, Perry, Wilkinson, Chapple, Lewis, Macfall, Christopher Jones, Davidson, Hadson, Harris, Leaver, Rapson, Mrs Teagal, Nurse Marchant, Doble, Emery, Teak, Jackson, Smith and Clarke.

Matron Barras, who was matron of the Shepton Mallet Military Hospital during the First World War.

Commercial Road. The police station and Court House were erected in 1857. On the left cars are parked outside Gunning's Garage.

Six
Recreation

Shepton Mallet Excelsior Band, 1924. The bandmaster was Mr H. Rowsell and his son is pictured in the front on the left.

The town swimming pool at Upper Charlton (on the Crown Industrial Estate) before the opening of the present pool at West Shepton. The old pool was originally a flooded quarry, and when seeking a new pool the Shepton Mallet Urban Council was offered a redundant waste-water reservoir adjacent to the Anglo Brewery where it remains today.

The 'new' Shepton swimming pool was opened May 1912 by Mr and Mrs J.W. Garton of the Brewery who provided the use of the pool at a nominal rate of 1s per annum. Messrs Dodimead were the contractors who undertook the conversion for a sum of £194. In 1933 the pool was sold to the Urban District Council for some £700. The pool remains open today.

Publican Daniel Blinman pictured outside the Victoria Inn, Board Cross with two of his grandchildren, Victor Smith, aged five and Stanley Mitchell aged three. Mr Blinman was a wheelwright by trade and made the Goat Cart pictured here. He also bred goats and pigs and used to sell home-made faggots in his shop within the pub.

Coronation day parade, *en-route* for the celebrations in Collett Park, with the Shepton Mallet Town Band, 2 June 1953. (Photograph courtesy of Mrs Maud Cleer).

Two entries for the Shepton Mallet Carnival, c. 1930. Freda Youdle on the horse as 'Pretty Maid' won first prize, and Frederick Youdle won second prize as 'Knight of Armour'. Freda said: 'They were separate entries really, but the horse loved the band, so dad had to hold her. Silk flags from cigarette packets were stitched around the horse blanket by Mum.'

Shepton Mallet Carnival 1929-1931. The only known name here is Annie Parker of Downside (extreme right, back row).

Assembling for the 1932 Shepton Carnival in Prince's Road. Harold Tinkler shelters under the umbrella and on the right is Meridith.

A church fête held in the Cricket Field at Townsend. In the back row is Mr Connock of Pilton, headmaster of Waterloo Road School.

A charabanc outing from the Crown Inn, parked in Longbridge. Those included are Mr and Mrs Tucker, Bailey, Jack Lumber, Hughie Thick, Mrs Hares, Eddie Dowling (landlord of the Crown Inn), Fred Gulliford, postman Rawling and wife, Jimmy Hodges, Crook, Charlie Hares and Mrs Hayter.

'Snail Eaters Banquet' at the Royal Oak, Commercial Road, December 1958. The demonstrator is Mr Fred Butler seen in the group above. First he removed the layer of slime from the mouth of the shell, stuck a pin into the snail and with a neat flick of the wrist, spiralled the snail out of its shell. Dipping it into vinegar he quickly swallowed it. Including: J. Pullen, Fred Butler, E. Wareham, L. Wells and Reakes.

Resplendent in their dashing uniforms the boys of one of Shepton Mallet's Drum and Fife Bands posed in 1905 for this photograph taken outside the Old Manor House in Leg Square, Shepton Mallet. Some of the names include Miles, Millard, Toogood and Baker. The photograph was taken by F.G. Steggles of Shepton Mallet.

Kilver Street Silver Band outside Kilver Street School, c. 1930.

Charlton Inn's Annual Outing, 31 July 1921. At Kilver Street Hill all passengers, including children alighted at the bottom of the hill and the men had to push. However this did not happen on this trip as it was bound for Minehead.

Shepton Mallet Town Football Team (1922/23) outside the Bunch of Grapes. Including: Len Brooks, Stan Green, Art Baker, Fred Green, Sonny Green, Percy Hodges, Len Feltham, Stan Martin and Bill Marshman (Ken Moore's father).

Shepton Mallet Town Football Team 1932/33. From left to right, back row: F.E. Heal, A.A. Clarke, L. Maccaule, J. Tucker, A. Miles, E. Teagle, S. Woolard, Paterson, G. Dunford. Middle row: T. Dunkerton, P. Gane, B. White, Butler, G. Witcombe. Front row: H. Veasey, V. Moore, K. Sparkes, B. Moore. (photograph courtesy of Percy Gane)

The most successful season the club ever experienced was 1933/34. They were winners of the Frome and District League Cup, Cheddar Valley League Cup, Cheddar Valley Charity Cup and Cheddar Valley Knock-Out-Cup. During the season the team lost only one league game and had an undefeated home record. In the Cheddar Valley League the town played 18 games, won 14, drew 3, and lost 1. There were 70 goals for and 9 against. In the Frome and District League 20 games were played of which 19 were won and 1 was drawn. From left to right, back row: J.H. Ellicott, F.E. Neal (treasurer), V. Moore, A. Miles (vice-captain), J. Tucker, W. Brooks. Middle row including: H. Vezey, S. Dark, B. White, R. Durk, K.S. Sparkes (captain), W. Rabbits (trainer). Front row: B. Moore (secretary), T. Dunkerton, P. Gane, H. Drew, L. Macauley, T. Patterson, A.A. Clarke (chairman).

Shepton Mallet Town Football Team in fancy dress during the 1930s. Among those pictured are: F. Venner, Bill Hicks, Ern Davis, Jim Cable, Fred Youdle, P. Lear, Sid Dalimore, E. Crispin, Frank Davis, Bill Hayes, P. Miles, E. Thick, Bob Hockey, E. Hams, B. Trim and B. Haul.

The dancing Bear was a frequent and popular visitor to Shepton at the turn of the twentieth century. The bear was kept in the brewery outbuildings at Lower Lane – now in the grounds of Barren Down House.

Seven

The War Years

Field telephone being erected outside the Hare and Hounds Hotel during manoeuvres held at Measbury, 1911.

Staff of the Shepton Mallet Military Hospital, 1914-1918. At the front, centre, is Matron Barras.

Patients of the Military Hospital, Shepton Mallet, c. 1916.

The Market Cross decorated with flowers, ferns and holly wreaths as Shepton's shrine on Peace Celebration Day, 19 July 1919.

Royal Observer Corps, 11 October 1943. From left to right, standing: Arthur Angwin, Jo Williams, Cliff Bailey, Percy Jacobs, Alex Fry, Dennis Simons, Arthur Poles, Cecil Clifford, Harry Fish, ? Higgins, Roy Bowden. Sitting: Wallace Baker, Reg Moon, Reg Byrt, Sammy Samson, Darby Miller.

The Girls Training Corps (GTC) marching up High Street, 1948. From left to right, back row: Elizabeth Stock. Fifth row: Vera Parsons, Beryl Price. Fourth row: Joyce Denning. Third row: Joan Prince, Joyce Warr, Ruby Rossiter. Second row: Lil Davis, Pam Rowe, Mary Biggin. First row: Pam Witts, Kay Veasey, Pam Clifford. Front: Joan Smith.

Some 250 Guides and Scouts march down Town Street following the mid-Somerset Association of Boy Scouts' St George Day service at the parish church. The parade had set out from the Waterloo Road Schools and are seen on their return.

Eight
Special Occasions

Flags, banners and garlands of flowers in High Street to welcome the Prince and Princess of Wales, June 1909.

Left: Junction of Paul Street and High Street in readiness for the Royal visit, June 1909.
Right: Annie Godfrey's shop decorated for the Royal visit. 'We had it decorated for the Prince's visit,' wrote Annie, 'We had a lovely time and at night we illuminated it all over in green and red. You can imagine the effect on the roses. We did it all ourselves. Made the feathers and all the flowers and it was just about a fine success.'

Every street in the town was festooned with garlands, flags and flowers. This picture shows a view from Town Street, looking south.

More decorations in Town Street for the Royal visit, 1909.

The Charlton Inn was also busy preparing for the Royal visit in June 1909.

Volleys of cheers went up as the Prince and Princess of Wales strolled by the lake in Collett Park during June 1909. Greeted by the chairman of the Shepton Mallet Town Council, Mr Garton, the Prince then planted an oak tree by the lake to celebrate his visit.

Mr Garton, chairman of the Urban District Council, welcomes the Prince and Princess of Wales to Collett Park.

Annie Godfrey's shop, this time decorated for the Coronation of King George V and Queen Mary in 1910.

The mill at Leg Square with the Kings Arms Inn in the background decorated for the Coronation of King George V and Queen Mary, 1910.

Entrance to Collett Park decorated for the Jubilee.

Entrants form up in front of the Charlton Brewery float in readiness for the Jubilee parade. George Banks is the driver, with Fred Bank at the back, right.

Another entrant for the 1935 Jubilee parade lining up in Princes Road. From left to right: Ken Hurrel, Terry Linthorne, Eddie Dowling, Tom and June Ware (in the pram), Tom Dean, Arthur Tucker (small lad with bike), Ken Ware (in the boat), Henry Dunn, Les Corben.

Henry 'Sunny' Moon and his sister in the Jubilee Parade, 1935.

Ready to go! The Charlton Brewery entry for the Jubilee Parade at the gates of the Brewery. John and Mary Swain are at the front.

The winning entry for the Jubilee parade was Charlton Brewery's 'Beer is Best'. Driver George Banks and his brother Fred poses in front of the float.

Post Office Workers forming up for the Jubilee Parade in 1935. From left to right, back row: E. Richmond, Mr Grose, W. Richmond, R. Allen, R. Cooper, G. Male, H. Nunn. Front row: R. Bidmead, Mr Tanner, G. Newport, C. Tripp, S. Dallimore, T. Walshe, S. Mitchell. The boy stood up at the front, Ern Gould, used to work at Hobley's. The man on the left, Sid Higgins, lived at Longbridge, and the man in plain clothes, Bill Hayes, used to own the Bunch of Grapes pub.

Collett Day, June 1906. It was a memorable day for the town. Streets were decorated from end to end with garlands of flowers, flags and bunting, and everywhere banners with, 'Welcome to Mr and Mrs Collett', 'Health to Mr Collett', and 'Good Luck to you'.

Left: High Street decorated in readiness for Collett Day, June 1906. Pictured is Mr Joe Gare (grocer), leaning on his cycle. The Revd George Mitchell is the man in white shoes and straw hat, then headmaster of Waterloo Road School. On the right is the council dustman or 'scavenger' with his horse and cart.

Right: More decorations for the Royal visit in the High Street.

John Kyte Collett continued to add to his original gift – a lake, shelter and bandstand were added to the park until it finally included over thirteen acres of lawns, shrubbery's and flowerbeds.

Preparations for the visit of the Prince of Wales in the High Street, 1909.

The Hare and Hounds Hotel at the junction of High Street and Commercial Road.

Decorations for the royal visit in Town Street.

Over 2,000 school children from the town and surrounding villages marched to Collett Park to greet the royal visitors.

The Prince and Princess of Wales accompanied by Mr Garton, chairman, and Mr Nalder, clerk to the Urban District Council, June 1909.

The Prince of Wales planting an Oak Tree adjacent to the lake in Collett Park, June 1909.

Crowds gather around the lake at Collett Park to greet the Prince and Princes of Wales.

After Sunday school, children play on the swings in Collett Park, *c.* 1910.

Nine

A Changing Townscape

The cul-de-sac off Cowl Street was demolished to make way for modern flats during the early 1960s.

The new town centre, Shepton Mallet, August 1985. (Photograph taken by Mr David Walsh.)

Monmouth House at the southern end of Cowl Street. It is said that the Duke of Monmouth's men stayed there on their ill-fated advance on Bristol in 1685. It was swept away to make way for the Hillmead Flats development during the early 1960s.

The modern Hillmead Flats still under construction in the mid-1960s.

Draycott Road formed the southern boundary of the Hillmead development and was demolished in the early 1960s. On the left is Mr Amor's Pet Shop.

Left: Sales House, Draycot, once a mill and dye-houses which were later converted into a convent. It has now been turned into flats.

Right: The seventeenth century Beach House and mill at Draycott was also swept away when Hillmead was developed.

The Hare and Hounds Hotel at the junction of High Street and Commercial Road closed in the spring of 1962 and was demolished to make way for the Keymarket Store.

The new Keymarket Store was considered a triumph of modern architecture at the time.

The Market Place, Shepton Mallet just prior to redevelopment in the early 1970s.

Demolition opened up a completely new vista of the Market Place.

Town Street looking south. The shops on the left and right in the foreground were swept away to make way for a new relief road in the early 1970s.

Two views of the old Council Offices and Hall from Church Lane. The top photograph is taken just before demolition, whilst the bottom photograph is taken during the construction of the new centre.

Following the demolition of the Town Street properties, the wasteland become an impromptu car park for almost a decade before eventual redevelopment.

The main view of the town centre redevelopment site, including the cellared area of the old council offices.

Left: The Church Tower and Market Cross.
Right: The Council Offices in the Market Place, partially demolished during the town centre redevelopment.

The Regal Cinema enjoyed a short life as a public hall before finally falling victim to redevelopment. Messrs W.E. Chivers, who built the Regal in 1933, were the contractors responsible for its demolition in 1973. The site now forms part of Regal Road.

Several of the cottage shops in Peter Street were to be lost to the redevelopment. In this picture 'Dick' Male scrubs up his table outside the butchers' shop there.

Other shops on the south side of Peter Street were also demolished.

Ten
Around Shepton Mallet

Postcards and research by Richard Rainsford

View of Pilton from Curnhill showing the parish church with the Old Rectory behind and Shop Lane, leading up to Conduit Square. The chimneys of the old brewery can be seen behind the former Swan Inn (now the village stores). In the foreground is the roof of Bier House that was used to house the parish bier. In front of the church is Monks Mill (an early nineteenth-century building) with the former manorial mill behind – now reduced to a single storey building. On the front of the postcard is written, 'Can Evercreech equal this?'

The manor house was built by the Abbots of Glastonbury during the twelfth century and was given a new front during the eighteenth century. In 1539 it is recorded that the building contained a hall, chapel, dining room and eight chambers, as well as a kitchen, buttery, cellar, stables and outhouses. Also adjoining is a fourteenth-century dovecote.

The Abbots of Glastonbury built Pilton Barn during the fourteenth century to store produce from the Pilton Manor. It had a thatched roof that caught fire when struck by lightening in 1964. After years of neglect it is now being restored with a new roof of tiles. The barn is ornamented with cross-shaped openings on the north side (which was visible from the manor) and carvings symbolising the Evangelists in the gables.

Bread Street still retains many of its old houses, although Mulberry House has had its roof replaced by tiles and a new house has been built beside it, otherwise the street remains much the same as seen in this early postcard. At the road junction on the extreme right is the Long House, a former bakery that was built on a long narrow plot – hence its name.

View looking east from the North Wooton junction. The attractive paving beside the shop has gone, as has the enormous thermometer. The Crown Inn was originally the tap to the Swan Inn, which occupied the present shop. It was used by the grooms and servants who could not afford to stay in the Swan.

Edmund Clark built Westholme House during the eighteenth century. It occupies a fine site to the west of the village with views of Glastonbury Tor. Included in its attractive landscaped grounds is a lodge to the east, stables to the north, an ornamental lake and a Dower House to the south. Westholme has a separate tithing to Pilton and has an alternative name of Fulbrook. It mainly consists of a scatter of farms to the south of the house.

A view looking north from Mount Pleasant to Beales House and 'John Beales Hill', but who John was is unfortunately not known. Beales House is a fine gabled seventeenth century building, but its once well-tended garden has been reduced by the erection of new houses. Behind is another old cottage and the early nineteenth-century John Beales House. The trees on the skyline have now been replaced by houses and the view to Beales House is largely obscured by trees.

Conduit Square – looking north to Pilton Stores with the Crow Inn on the right. The village war memorial is in the foreground and the present post office behind it.

Burford House, Pilton.

Burford House was built as a country house in 1853 and is a fine example of its type. It occupies a delightful position in a valley north of Pilton village. The size of the house made it unsuitable for modern requirements and has been subdivided into three dwellings. A little further down the lane is Burford Farm, a much older building, possibly of medieval origins.

West Pennard is situated on the road midway between Shepton Mallet and Glastonbury and is attractively sited below the western end of Pennard Hill. The village consists of several parts, one along the main road, one around the church and a connecting street called New Town. The latter name may refer to a new settlement created in the middle ages. The buildings pictured still largely exists, although the number of bicycles has probably reduced!

The Red Lion (or Lion) as it is now called is an historic building which still retains much of its old charm. Whilst most of the buildings remain, the main road has changed considerably and no longer has a dirt surface.

West Pennard church stands at the end of a no-through road next to the village school. It is an attractive, mainly perpendicular style building with a churchyard-cross located immediately to the south. The village school is still thankfully in use, although the clothes of the children have changed somewhat. In the picture they are walking along the paved footpath which leads to Pennard Farm.

Breach Lane is located to the south of West Pennard and leads to West Bradley. The house on the left was built in Victorian times and is called The Elms. Many of the trees in the picture (particularly the Elms) have now gone.

Evercreech is a large village situated on the south side of Shepton Mallet. The picture shows Weymouth Road which leds southwest towards Weston Town. The large building on the left is the Brewers Arms, and the cottages in the foreground were demolished to create its car park. The wall on the right was also removed to accommodate a commercial garage.

A large group of children pose for the camera on the open space in front of the parish church and also at the foot of the old cross that is said to have been moved from the churchyard. The two metal pumps in the foreground have unfortunately been removed and replaced by an ornamental rockery.

The picture shows the other side of the space in front of the church. It was one of the commercial hearts of the village until the late twentieth century as the shops on the left illustrate. The space is still used for car parking although the type of vehicles has changed!

Victoria Square is the present commercial heart of Evercreech and still has a number of shops around it. Unfortunately the attractive shop front has been altered although the buildings are largely the same.

Oxford Street is located to the south of the Evercreech parish church. Most of the buildings remain the same and it is only the unsurfaced road and lack of footpaths which reveal the age of the picture.

Kale Street, Batcombe. Batcombe prospered from the late middle ages through to the sixteenth century from the cloth trade. It still retains some traces of this prosperity in the early twentieth century as is seen in the various shops and trades which survived in Kale Street.

Batcombe church is famous as a fine example of perpendicular style architecture, particularly its west tower which was completed around 1540. On the west-side are six carved flying angels similar to those at Chewton Mendip church.

Ditcheat is a large village built around the churchyard of its parish church and the grounds of its former manor house. The village has a number of attractive buildings and still retains its village inn and shop. One of the characteristics of the village is the use of brick in several of its buildings due to a local brickyard operating in the late eighteenth and early nineteenth century.

Ditcheat parish church is a superb, mainly perpendicular style structure that dominates the village. It is cruciform in shape with a central tower and a good collection of gargoyles, 'hunky punks' and other carvings adorning the outside. Inside the visitor is not disappointed thanks to Ralph Hopton, Lord of the Manor who refurbished the church in 1610.

Doulting village was formerly owned by the Paget family of East Cranmore and was largely rebuilt in the late nineteenth and early twentieth century to designs by G.J. Skipper, an architect from Norwich. A disastrous fire that occurred on Sunday 2 May 1852, when nine dwellings were destroyed, probably prompted the rebuilding. The local paper reported, 'The fire was discovered burning on the roof of Mr E. Witcombe's house, when scarcely larger than a man's hat. In a few minutes it extended itself over the whole of the building, and a brisk wind prevailing, the houses on the opposite side of the street were soon in flames. Until the arrival of the engines from Shepton Mallet, the fire continued to spread, and for a time the whole village was lucky to have escaped destruction. Sparks from a boiler flue falling on a thatched roof was the cause of this calamity. With one exception, the parties were enabled to save their furniture, and there being no empty houses in the place, the Revd J. Fussell at once threw open the vicarage house for the reception of all who were thus rendered homeless. Very little property was insured.'

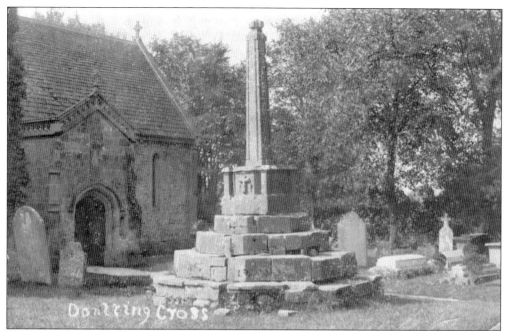

Historically the village of Doulting is very important, being the place where St Aldhelm died on 25 May 709 whilst on a journey from Sherborne to Malmsbury. He is said to have built the Saxon predecessor to the present church which was largely rebuilt in the middle ages and drastically remodelled in the mid-nineteenth century. The churchyard cross is one of the best in the locality and dates from the late fifteenth century. It has instruments of Passion carved around its base.

Doulting manor was granted to Glastonbury Abbey by Inne, King of the West Saxons in 688-726. During the fifteenth century the Abbey had a superb barn built to store produce from the estate. This is located to the south of the village, beside the manor farm and it is still used for agricultural purposes. It is one of the finest barns built by Glastonbury Abbey and has two gabled entrances instead of the normal one. A good view of the barn can be obtained from the adjoining road.

The manor of Doulting was particularly desirable because of its supply of freestone, which was used to build both Wells Cathedral and Glastonbury Abbey. Many abandoned quarries can be found around the village and the stone is still extracted. Most of the quarries lie to the north of the village near the hamlet of Chelynch. The picture shows the former New Inn, now the Poachers Pocket and its adjoining cottages.

Cranmore, named after a 'cranes mere' or pond, consists of two settlements – east and west. Its school, located in Cranmore Hall, now dominates East Cranmore, whereas West Cranmore is an attractive village grouped around its pond. To the north of the pond is the Strode Arms Inn, whilst to the south is Manor Farm and a group of thatched cottages.

Southill House is an impressive classical style building standing in its own grounds, south of West Cranmore. For some 200 years it was the home of the Strode family, lords of the manor and was built around 1720. During the Second World War it was the local headquarters of the British Resistance Organization; a secret underground unit trained to resist the threat of invasion during 1939-1945.

Dean is small hamlet located on the A361 between East and West Cranmore. It was originally the home of the Strode family in the seventeenth century and their house, now a farm still survives. The hamlet has suffered from the need for road 'improvements' and buildings on the south side of the road have been largely demolished. The chapel still exist however, and the former garage is awaiting conversion to an alternative use.

The Paget family built Cranmore Tower, located on the crest of the hill north of Dean in 1862-1965 to a design by T.H. Wyatt. It is an Italianate structure and was mainly used as a scenic place for the family to take 'teas'. They would drive up in a carriage from Cranmore Hall. A tower keeper's cottage formerly existed but is now ruinous. The tower has subsequently been converted into a private dwelling.

Oakhill Brewery, c. 1914. The village of Oakhill some three miles north of Shepton Mallet grew up around its brewery during the eighteenth century. It reached its height during the late nineteenth century, but unfortunately a disastrous fire occurred in 1925 and activity was reduced to malting only. The old maltings have now been converted, appropriately as a brewery.

It is said that no less than 500 people went on this outing organized by the Co-op in 1925. From left to right: Jack Moon, ? Bevan, Len Bevan, Fred Balch, Evie Martin, -?-, Gertie Lambert, -?-, Charlie Swain, Bob Baker, -?-.

Oakhill Rational Cub parade.

The Bakehouse at Zion Hill, Oakhill 1908. From left to right: D. Lovell, Mr King, Mr Drew, F. Rogers.

The Somerton and District Gospel Mission Van was a frequent visitor to Shepton Mallet and the surrounding villages.

Oakhill WI taking part in the Coronation Parade depicting the coronation of Queen Elizabeth, 1953. Including: M. Reeves, P. Penny, L. Reeves, Mary Reeves, J, Chislett, B. Pollitt, M. Bevan, E. Trippick, G. Rabbits and E. Herridge.

'It was the smallest choir to enter the Bath Music Festival competition of some sixteen entrants, around 1955. We sang an old Somerset Folk song, *I gave my love an apple*. Although this was unaccompanied we still won the cup!' (quote from Mary Reeves). From left to right, back row: M. Reeves, R. Ridler, R. Tilke, J. Gilling, E. Herridge, M. Lander, E. Trippick, G. Rabbits. Front row: P. Gefferies, J. Chislett, L. Reeves, M. Reeves, B. Pollitt, M. Bevan, N. Fear, J. Voisey

The Age of Steam – a traction engine, *c.* 1890.

Joe Gregory and Dave Bryant with an early Oakhill Brewery lorry.

Croscombe, some $2\frac{1}{2}$ miles west of Shepton Mallet was once a thriving little 'town' with some 2,000 inhabitants. It was the days of the 'Golden Fleece' for a community basking in the wealth of the West Country Woollen Industry. Countless sheep grazed on the steep sleights above the village. As with many other parts of the Mendip Hills, the fast flowing streams were much sought after as motive power for numerous mills that straddled the river. It was said that Croscombe was as big as Wells and as important as Shepton Mallet. Edward 1 granted a Market Charter in 1283, with an annual fair to be held on Lady Day each year. The village fair was a regular event and an attempt was made to revive it in 1920.

View of the main road through Croscombe with the present post office in the foreground. In the middle distance is the village cross, a reminder of the former market statue of the village. It was almost knocked doen in the early twentieth century as a highway improvement but thanks to local resistance was saved. Behind is the present Bull Terrier Inn (formely the Rose and Crown.)

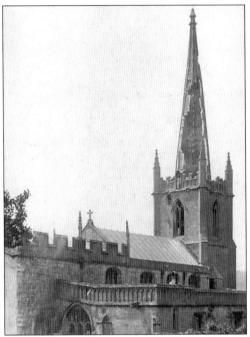

Left: Croscombe church is one of the best in the area. It has a wealth of historic features and a delightfully restored interior. The west tower and spire date from the fourteenth century, but the majority of the building was erected during the fifteenth century. The outside displays a number of grotesque carvings known locally as 'hunky punks'. Inside, the church is dominated by fittings installed by the Fortescue family (lords of the manor) in the early seventeenth century. These include a very fine pulpit with its tester dated 1616, the wooden screen surmounted by the coat of arms of James 1, the side screens, reader's desk and some of the box pews.

Right: St Mary's church, Croscombe after the steeple was struck by lightening during a storm in 1936.

A prize winning entry at the village fair in May 1920 – 'Britannia'.

Croscombe School outing, c. 1924.

'Off to Weston-Super-Mare.' Croscombe outing of workers from Dulcote Quarry, 1919.

Dinder, Nr Wells.

Dinder is a delightful estate village located in the valley of the River Sheppey between Croscombe and Dulcote. It is dominated by Dinder House, which stands in spacious grounds immediately south of the village church. The picture shows Riverside, an attractive range of buildings that overlook a leat diverted from the River Sheppey.

Dulcot Hill, Near Wells.

Harvey Barton's Series.

Dulcote takes it name from the original name of the River Sheppey, 'Doulting Water'. It is dominated by Dulcote Hill to the south, an outcrop of carboniferous limestone. The other distinctive feature of Dulcote is its fountain fed by a natural artesian well which raises water up from underground sources below the Mendip Hills.